GW00721978

Bee Three Publishing is an imprint of Books By Boxer
Published by
Books By Boxer, Leeds, LS13 4BS UK
Books by Boxer (EU), Dublin D02 P593 IRELAND
© Books By Boxer 2024 All Rights Reserved
MADE IN CHINA
ISBN: 9781915410382

This book is produced from responsibly sourced paper to ensure forest management

Men can often be found with a messy tangle of hair on their chins and are often too stubborn to shave...

UNFORTUNATELY, SOMETIMES THAT STUBBORNNESS CAN BE FATAL.

Hans Staininger, a politician from the 16th-century, was proud of his 7 foot beard and refused to chop it.

One day, he tripped over his facial hair - snapping his neck in the process!

MEN WILL GO TO GREAT LENGTHS TO AVOID ASKING FOR DIRECTIONS.

If a woman finds herself taking a wrong turn, she'll do the smart thing and ask a pedestrian the way to her destination.

However, only 6% of men would ask for directions or check a map if lost, and

WILL TRAVEL AN EXTRA 18 MILES PER YEAR TO AVOID ADMITTING THEY'RE WRONG!

In 2000, during a beautiful summer in Colorado, a 34 year old masonry contractor had a bright idea to keep his pesky pup in his yard.

DESPITE NEVER HAVING EXPERIENCE AS AN ELECTRICIAN

he decided to go all out and build himself an electric fence.
At first, things worked out smoothly, however one day he went into his yard to pick some tomatoes, accidentally touched the fence, and got a shock that would leave him sizzling!

Danger
High Voltage

SEE, THE PROBLEM IS THAT GOD GIVES MEN

A BRAIN AND A PENIS

AND ONLY ENOUGH BLOOD TO RUN ONE AT A TIME

-Robin Williams

HOW NOT TO CLEAN WINDOWS

WHEN LIGHTING FIREWORKS

women tend to place them securely in the ground first before lighting them.

Men however, like to

PLACE THEM SECURELY BETWEEN THEIR BUTTCHEEKS!

Between this and juggling with grenades, It's no wonder over 50 men have been reported to have fatally blown themselves to smithereens with explosions!

You've invented the world's first overcoat parachute but

HOW DO YOU TEST YOUR SUCCESSFUL NEW INVENTION?

Don't be like Franz Reichelt, who decided that the best way to test his new invention was to

JUMP FROM THE TOP OF THE EIFFEL TOWER

-only to find that his invention actually didn't work and plummeted to his death.

How many pallets does it take to change a lightbulb?

In a Japanese logistics warehouse, a worker was tasked to change a lightbulb 10 meters high.

In an act of genius stupidity, he took it upon himself to stack a rickety pile of pallets onto his forklift then convince a co-worker to forklift him to the ceiling. The wooden structure collapsed...

NOW THE WAREHOUSE WORKER IS IN A HIGHER PLACE...

When strapping yourself to some elastic and plummeting to the ground from a great height, you'd think it smart to at least

CHECK YOU'RE NOT GOING TO HIT THE GROUND FIRST!

60 unfortunate men decided not to check before their thrill-seeking bungee jump.

(A mistake they can't bounce back from.)

WHEN WORKING WITH ROBOTS, ALWAYS ENSURE THE OFF SWITCH IS ACTIVATED.

Otherwise you may find yourself like Kenji Urada, who was pushed by a malfunctioning arm of the robot he was working on, into a grinder.

He fell to a very grisly death, becoming one of the first people to be killed by a robot.

A 33 year old man from England was found dead in his home after calling himself an ambulance, and had suffered a stabbing.

However no assailant was found, and no crime had been committed. The man had actually stabbed himself!

You see, he had recently bought a new coat,

AND WONDERED IF IT WAS STAB-PROOF...

The answer was no.

WHEN A WOMAN SAYS

"WHAT?"

IT'S NOT BECAUSE SHE DIDN'T
HEAR YOU.

SHE'S JUST GIVING YOU A CHANCE
TO FIX WHAT YOU SAID.

-Unknown

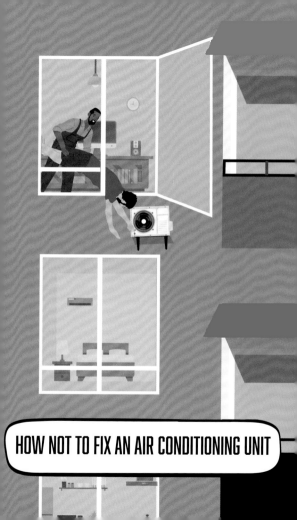

HOW NOT TO FIX AN AIR CONDITIONING UNIT

WOMEN LIKE THE COMFORT OF THEIR OWN HOME...

and entertainment comes easy to them in the form of a good book or TV show.

Men however, are thrill-seekers, and will go to the most dangerous places on earth to stop feeling bored. 25 outgoing idiots have

DIED IN THE NAME OF BOREDOM,

in ways like dehydrating in the desert and sinking on a manmade raft.

A 29 YEAR OLD PERSONAL TRAINER DIED FROM CAFFEINE TOXICITY

after ingesting the equivalent of 200 cups of coffee in caffeine powder.

He attempted to weigh around 60 milligrams of the powder, but used a scale which ranged from 2 grams to 5,000 grams...

WHAT A WEIGH TO DIE!

If an outdoorsy weekend is said to be ruined by torrential storms, most women might reschedule for better weather.

Men would pack a light jumper and embrace the rain, but maybe that's why

MEN ARE FOUR TIMES MORE LIKELY TO BE STRUCK BY LIGHTNING.

CAN'T GET AN UBER?

we don't suggest

JOYRIDING IN A SHOPPING CART TO GET HOME QUICKER.

2 men decided to take a shopping cart home after a night out but on their unconventional journey,

they hit a car at high speed,

CATAPULTING THEM OUT OF THE CART AND INTO THE ROAD WITH SERIOUS, LIFE ENDING INJURIES.

THINK TWICE BEFORE YOU GRAB A CAN OF DEODORANT TO CONTROL YOUR MANLY ODOR.

A man from England covered his entire body in deodorant at a minimum of twice a day after becoming obsessed with smelling fresh.

However,

HE SUFFERED A HEART ATTACK

due to a build-up of the deodorant gases in his body, after continually spraying himself in an unventilated room!

SKATEBOARDING IS A POPULAR HOBBY.

Unfortunately it's not one free of morbid stupidity.

IN 2014, 3 PEOPLE DIED FROM 'SKITCHING'.

Skitching is the act of hitching a ride by holding onto a moving motor vehicle while riding a skateboard, bike or roller skates.

If the rain cancels your BBQ plans we suggest to move your event to another weekend instead.

DON'T ATTEMPT TO LIGHT AND USE YOUR BBQ INDOORS.

This will lead to carbon monoxide poisoning which is very likely to end in an untimely death.

Maybe just get a takeout instead...

This should seem like common sense but...

NEXT TIME YOU ARE DARED TO EAT A NEWT... DON'T.

In 1979, an American college student was dared to swallow a newt.

Unfortunately the newt he chose to swallow had

SKIN THAT PRODUCES A STRONG TOXIN

which very quickly sent him into cardiac arrest.

HUMANS – 0, NEWT – 1.

BEHIND EVERY GREAT MAN

IS A WOMAN ROLLING HER EYES.

-Jim Carrey

HOW NOT TO CUT DOWN BRANCHES

If you want to put something up your backside, who are we to tell you otherwise?

However, if you put it

SO FAR UP THAT YOU END UP IN THE ER,

you might want to reconsider.

From sex toys and drugs to jars and writing implements, approximately 4,000 Americans are hospitalized each year due to

'FOREIGN OBJECTS' LODGED UP THEIR RECTUM

- and 77.8% of cases were men!

FEELING SNACKISH?

Maybe avoid that ominous looking
vending machine next to the stairwell.

VENDING MACHINES ON AVERAGE KILL 10-13 PEOPLE EACH YEAR BY TOPPLING OVER,

crushing their poor, hungry,
unsuspecting victim.

In the late 90s, one couple decided to cure their late night boredom

BY TAKING A FEW STICKS OF DYNAMITE ON A MIDNIGHT DRIVE...

Unfortunately due to the couple's intoxicated state

THEY FORGOT TO ROLL DOWN THE WINDOWS TO THROW OUT THE DYNAMITE,

leading to disastrous consequences.

Next time, might we suggest a game of Scrabble?

A love of sports is something shared by many, however this passion could prove to be deadly.

EACH YEAR SPECTATORS DIE FROM BEING HIT BY GOLF BALLS, CRICKET BALLS, RACING RALLY CARS OR MOTORCYCLES.

Next time, stay home and watch from the safety of the couch and TV screen.

In many countries, it is customary to

FIRE BULLETS INTO THE AIR IN CELEBRATION.

As bullets fall back to the ground after being fired, they gain velocity and can

EASILY PENETRATE SKIN AND THE SKULL.

Next time Uncle Sam is feeling trigger happy, maybe convince him to have a celebratory beer instead.

(Or at least wear a helmet!)

Whilst eating carrots will improve your overall eye health, it won't enable you to see in the dark, so we don't recommend

GUZZLING 10 GALLONS OF CARROT JUICE TO INDUCE NIGHT VISION.

You will only be victim to a Vitamin A overdose, causing you to

SUFFER BRIGHT YELLOW SKIN AND SEVERE LIVER DAMAGE,

such as the unfortunate Basil Brown from Croydon, England.

In 2015, a German man died after a botched robbery attempt...

But how did he die? A piece of metal shrapnel hit him in the head after using a

HOMEMADE BOMB TO BLOW UP A CONDOM DISPENSER...

Shame he wasn't wearing the right kind of protection.

THIS FACT MAY LEAVE YOU THINKING MEN ARE ONTO SOMETHING...

when their bachelor boudoir beds are adorned with nothing apart from a single sheet and sad, lonely pillow.

OVER 10,000 PEOPLE HAVE DIED FROM ACCIDENTAL SUFFOCATION AND STRANGULATION IN BED!

WHAT'S THE DIFFERENCE
BETWEEN A SMART MAN AND
A STUPID MAN?

NOTHING...

THEY BOTH THINK THEY KNOW
EVERYTHING.

-Unknown

THERE'S 'DANGER OF ELECTROCUTION' SIGNS FOR A REASON.

Though women will typically heed the bright yellow omen of death, **MEN ARE EITHER BLIND TO THE SIGNS OR TAKE IT AS A CHALLENGE.**

Breaking into a power grid, trespassing onto railway lines and stealing live wires are just some of the dumb ways **23 DIMWITS ZAPPED THEIR LIFE AWAY!**

In 2007, an intoxicated 23 year old male decided to

HANG OUT WITH BEARS IN A SERBIAN ZOO.

Wandering nude into the bear's enclosure, he was quite expectedly

MAULED TO DEATH BY TWO BEARS,

and was found naked along with many beer cans...

HOW NOT TO USE LADDERS

HOW NOT TO CHOP WOOD

2 Californian men nearly took a plunge to their death **AFTER PLAYING POKÉMON GO.** The app, which makes you travel to collect Pokémon, had **LED THEM TO A CRUMBLING 100 FOOT CLIFF,** off which they both promptly fell but luckily survived!

Next time Grandma says 'He's a growing boy - fix him another plate' heed this cautionary tale of King Adolf Frederick of Sweden - notably

THE KING THAT ATE HIMSELF TO DEATH.

Though if we do say, a last meal of lobster, caviar, kippers & champagne followed by an alleged 14 selma buns served with hot milk - does sound rather nice...

In the US, the workforce has a pretty even split between men & women. Men do however champion in one thing...

ON-THE-JOB FATALITIES, OF WHICH MEN ACCOUNT FOR 94%!

Clement Vallandigham, an American lawyer, argued his case a bit too successfully when he

ACCIDENTALLY SHOT HIMSELF

while acting out to the jury how his clients' alleged murder victim had actually shot themselves during a court case in 1871.

HARD TO ARGUE WITH THAT EVIDENCE...

THE SIGHT OF A WOMAN'S CLEAVAGE

REDUCES A MAN'S ABILITY TO THINK CLEARLY BY

50% ...
PER BOOB.

-Unknown

HOW NOT TO CUT HEDGES

A study shows that out of 21,000 forensic autopsies,

39 PEOPLE HAD DIED FROM NATURAL CAUSES WHILE HAVING SEX.

That being said, only 2 of the 39 people were women.

MEN, NEXT TIME YOU WANT TO GET DOWN AND DIRTY...

maybe check your life insurance is valid first?

A MAN IN BRAZIL WENT OUT WITH A BANG AFTER HE DECIDED TO DISASSEMBLE AN RPG.

First, the man tried to run over the grenade back and forth, and when that didn't work, took to pounding it with a sledgehammer!

THE RPG DID DISASSEMBLE - BY BLOWING UP!

It took the man out, along with six cars and a repair shop... 14 more RPGs were found nearby, believed to have been collected for scrap metal!

77% of people who enjoy golf as a hobby or profession are men, which may not be so surprising given the sport's reputation as male dominated. What may surprise you is the level of

GOLF-COURSE-RELATED INJURIES.

One unlucky example of this is a teenager who was

PIERCED IN THE HEART BY HIS OWN CLUB,

when it snapped after he slammed it against a bench, following a poor round on a New York golf course.

Usually any form of death that has been recorded throughout history is no laughing matter - however in this case it absolutely is.

DEATH FROM LAUGHTER

is a rare occurrence in which the victim literally laughs themselves to point of cardiac arrest or asphyxiation. Victims include 3rd-century BC Greek philosopher Chrysippus, and Alex Mitchell, from 1970's England, who

DIED AFTER LAUGHING FOR AN ALLEGED 25 MINUTES CONTINUOUSLY

following an episode of 'The Goodies'!

Some say men can't multitask -
they may be right.

During an attempted burglary of a bicycle
store in California, 1997, in effort to keep
both hands free while on the store's roof,
the thief held a flashlight in his mouth.
Unfortunately this

FLASHLIGHT ENDED UP KILLING HIM BY SMASHING THROUGH HIS SKULL

after he lost his balance and fell face first
onto the floor.

On a sunny beach in North Carolina, 1997, a man decided to dig a hole in the sand, and then sit in it for fun.

THE HOLE WAS 8 FOOT DEEP, AND COLLAPSED, TRAPPING THE MAN INSIDE!

Beach-goers tried to dig him out, but only when special equipment arrived was he pulled back to the surface - a gritty demise indeed!

A Japanese man lost his life after his beloved hamster, Aiko (translated to Little Love) bit him.

It turns out that his

'LITTLE LOVE' WAS THE CAUSE OF HIS DEATH,

causing the man to have an adverse reaction to a protein the hamster's saliva

RESULTING IN HIM DYING FROM ANAPHYLACTIC SHOCK.

An old man from the UK wanted to ease his wife's neck pain, so he created a DIY device out of wood and rope to help apply traction to her neck.

He tested it out first, and lo and behold,

ACCIDENTALLY HUNG HIMSELF,

as his contraption turned out to be a DIY gallow! Maybe just use muscle ointment instead?

LIFE IS HARD...

BUT IT'S HARDER IF YOU'RE STUPID.

- Michael Crichton

SECURITY CHECK

Everyone is prone to a sticky situation sometime in their lives...

Take superglue,

PERFECT FOR CRACKED POTTERY, NOT SO PERFECT FOR GLUING YOUR EYES SHUT.

Despite warnings on the packaging,

MORE MEN THAN WOMEN GLUE THEIR EYES SHUT,

with 105 patients in total during 3 months.

Many people think man flu is a myth, but let me tell you, it's real!

Researchers from both Hong Kong and the USA have found that men have a much higher risk of hospital admission and even

DEATH FROM THE COMMON FLU.

This is because men

HAVE A WEAKER IMMUNE SYSTEM THAN WOMEN,

making the symptoms worse!

You might remember getting a wedgie from a school bully or your friends trying to prank you, but nobody could ever expect

'DEATH BY WEDGIE' BEING WRITTEN ON AN AUTOPSY REPORT!

This became true for an Oklahoma man, who, during a fight with his stepson, was given an 'atomic wedgie', and was

STRANGLED BY HIS OWN UNDERWEAR

that he was wearing at the time.

In their pastime, men will often kick back with a game of FIFA or Call of Duty on their games console. Gaming: a fun and harmless hobby you may think - but 24 people have

DIED FROM PLAYING VIDEO GAMES

- and 23 of those people were men! The main cause of these deaths are

CARDIAC ARREST AND BLOOD CLOTS - CAUSED BY EXTENSIVE GAMING SESSIONS.

In 1989, a 60 year old man, who was celebrating his 25 year anniversary working at a brewery, went missing when he left the pub he was celebrating in.

HE'D CREPT BACK INTO HIS WORKPLACE, STRIPPED NAKED, AND JUMPED INTO 35,000 PINTS OF BEER.

His clothes were found beside the vat the next morning.

87% of women change their underwear everyday, however, more than 1 in 5 men say they can get away with

WEARING THE SAME PAIR OF BOXERS TWO DAYS IN A ROW.

This is because men find convenient hacks to prolong having to wash their undies...

INSIDE OUT AND BACK TO FRONT ARE JUST TWO COMBINATIONS

to keep them away from the machine!

A man was fatally injured in Manchester, UK, after climbing onto the bonnet of his friend's car and riding at speed, before falling off.

A WOMAN WOULD GET INTO THE CAR FIRST.

MEN LOVE A BIT OF DIY -

but this could be the reason that around 4,800 people (mainly males) annually are admitted into hospital due to

POWER DRILL RELATED ACCIDENTS.

Do us all a favor and stick to a manual screwdriver!

IF STUPID WAS A SPORT,

I WOULD BE

SURROUNDED

BY

CHAMPIONS.

-Unknown

HOW NOT TO PAINT WINDOW FRAMES

NATURE DOESN'T SEEM TO BE ON MEN'S SIDE!

Whether this is due to men going outside in all weathers (something most women would rather not do), or just being in the wrong place at the wrong time - trees seem to have a vendetta against the male species!

OUT OF ALL ACCIDENTAL INJURIES CAUSED BY FALLING TREES, 76% WERE MEN!

YOU WOULD THINK THAT MEN WOULD HAVE GOTTEN USED TO USING THEIR ZIPPER BY NOW.

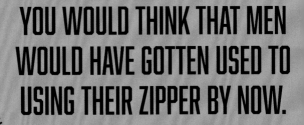

But zipper injuries are cropping up left, right and center!

Did you know, according to a 2013 study

OVER 2,000 MEN IN THE USA WERE ADMITTED INTO THE ER ANNUALLY...

for zipper-related injuries? Ouch!

HOW NOT TO FIX A WINDOW

Everyone loves to dip their toes in the ocean, but not everyone wants to swim with the fish!

Either sharks love male flesh, or men are just fools in the ocean.

One thing is certain though,

MEN ARE 9 TIMES MORE LIKELY TO BE ATTACKED BY A SHARK...

and 93% of shark attack victims are male!

Women, when feeling frisky, will use a reputable product to satisfy her needs.

Men, however, will take any item that could do the job, and get to work!

4 FATALITIES (ALL MALE)

have occurred when something other than a sex toy was used.

One in particular, found his demise when he used both a

VACUUM CLEANER AND A HAIRDRYER TO MASTURBATE.

A BRAZILIAN PRIEST TIED HIMSELF TO 1,000 HELIUM-FILLED BALLOONS

and floated over the ocean in a bid to raise money for a new parish.

He set off, helmet, parachute, and balloons in tow - but 8 hours later, he went off the grid, and

BALLOONS WERE SEEN SCATTERED AND FLOATING IN THE SEA

two days after, with no sign of the priest.

In Argentina, 2017, a man faced trial for carrying an illegal weapon. He was let free though. Why?

Because the weapon he was concealing down his pants had

SHOT HIM IN THE TESTICLES, RESULTING IN HIM LOSING HIS FAMILY JEWELS

and his job as a security guard where he was given the weapon in the first place!

WHAT YOU NEED TO KNOW ABOUT MEN AND WOMEN:

WOMEN ARE CRAZY, MEN ARE STUPID.

BUT THE **MAIN REASON** WOMEN ARE CRAZY IS BECAUSE

MEN ARE STUPID.

-Unknown

HOW NOT TO WELD METAL

When it comes to mowing one's yard, you might think 'That's a man's job', and you'd be right -

90% OF LAWNMOWERS ARE OWNED BY GARDEN-LOVING MEN...

That being said, with those statistics and the knowledge that men will mess around making crop circles for entertainment -

70 AMERICANS ANNUALLY ARE KILLED IN LAWNMOWER RELATED INCIDENTS,

and you're more likely to die by lawnmower than you are lightning!

Tired of having his workshop broken into, a 60 year old Brazilian man tried to take the law into his own hands and built a security device which ended in his demise. Made from copper wires and a firearm,

THE MAN MADE A BOOBY-TRAP TO CATCH THE CRIMINALS.

However, the burglars never showed up that night, and, on entering his workshop the next morning,

THE OLD MAN WAS SHOT DOWN BY HIS UNFORTUNATELY SUCCESSFUL INVENTION!

Men have an obsession with farting. Women, on the other hand, tend to find farting crude, and would die of embarrassment if they farted in front of company. That being said,

A MAN ACTUALLY DIED FROM SMELLING HIS OWN FARTS!

With a diet of mainly cabbage and beans, and no ventilation in his bedroom,

THE MAN SUFFOCATED TO DEATH WHILE SLEEPING.

His rescuers weren't without harm either, three were sick from the stench, and another had to be hospitalized!

Jack Daniel (yes, the distillery legend)

DIED RESULTING FROM A KICK TO HIS OFFICE SAFE.

In 1911, Jack kicked his safe in frustration
when he couldn't remember
the combination. An infection in his toe
was the result from such a kick, which

LED TO BLOOD POISONING AND AN UNTIMELY DEATH.

Ouch.

On a busy Californian interstate in 2021, two men had a car crash. **WITHOUT MOVING THEIR CARS TO THE SIDE OF THE ROAD, THEY GOT OUT OF THEIR CARS... AND ARGUED?!** Stood in the lanes of traffic and squabbling about who's fault the accident was, neither of the men saw the oncoming Mini Cooper which swerved the wreck, but collided with both men, proving fatal.

MORAL OF THE STORY, GET TO SAFETY BEFORE LASHING OUT AT ONE ANOTHER!

In 2017, a German man who'd found idiotic courage through booze, decided to bust open a train station's ticket machine, to make a few quick bucks.

HE SPRAYED CANS OF AEROSOL GAS INTO THE MACHINE, THEN IGNITED IT,

causing him to arrive at his final destination -

DEATH!

Whilst women sit and read stories of crazy thrillseekers, men are out there actually doing it!

A Californian man crossed the line when he

TIED A GOLF CART TO A VEHICLE USING A GARDEN HOSE.

Intended to be a bit of harmless fun, the man piloted the golf cart and was having a blast, right until the cart swerved over the line,

CRASHING INTO A TRUCK AND ENDING HIS LIFE INSTANTLY.

A man in Florida met his demise when he

WENT ON THE HUNT FOR... FRISBEES?

(A common occurrence, apparently.)

Wanting to find Frisbees to sell,
the man entered a lake that had

CLEAR WARNING SIGNS

and you guessed it!

HE GOT DEVOURED BY AN ALLIGATOR!

I'M NOT SAYING YOU'RE STUPID;

YOU JUST HAVE

BAD LUCK

WHEN IT COMES TO THINKING.

-Unknown

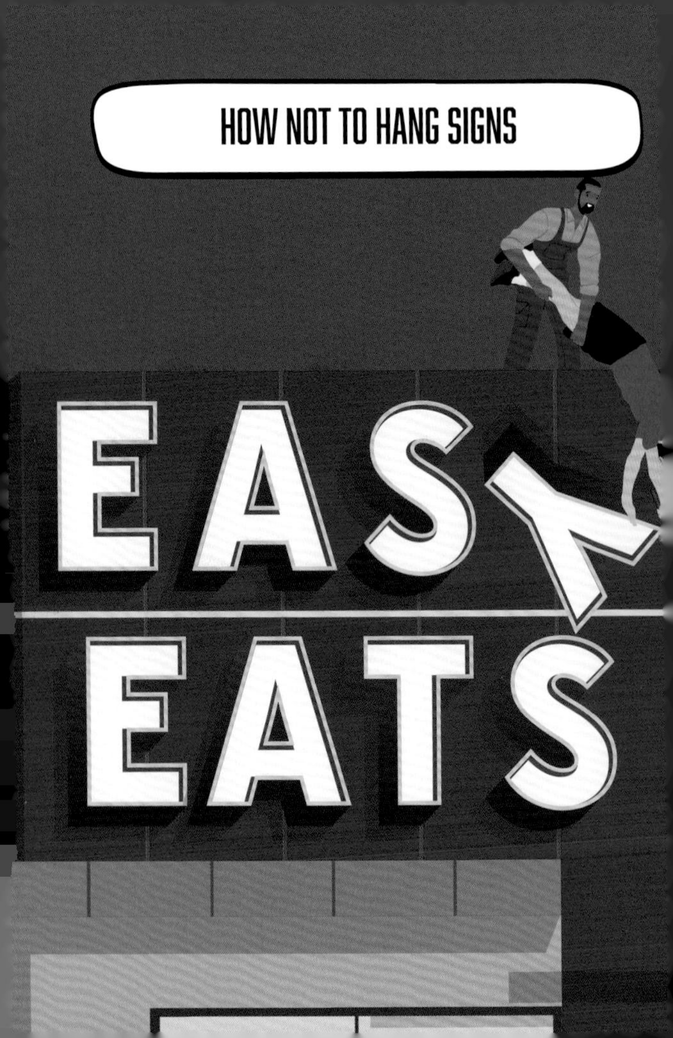
HOW NOT TO HANG SIGNS
EASY
EATS

In Lithuania, two draw bridges were lifted for their annual 'Sea Festival', where ships parade on the water.

WHILE THE BRIDGES WERE UP,

one man decided this would be a great challenge for his rental SUV and attempted to jump over the bridge.

Before the jump, he hesitated, and he and

HIS RENTAL CAR ENDED UP SWIMMING WITH THE FISH!

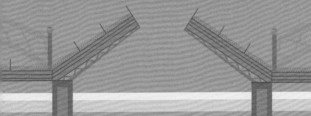

THE CHANCES OF A PET SNAKE KILLING ITS OWNER ARE 1 IN 1,500,000.

This statistic definitely becomes more likely when you decide to kiss them... As in the case of an 18 year old teen from Florida, who decided to

KISS A VENOMOUS COTTONMOUTH SNAKE

to entertain his friends. Thankfully the teen recovered and hopefully learned a safer party trick.

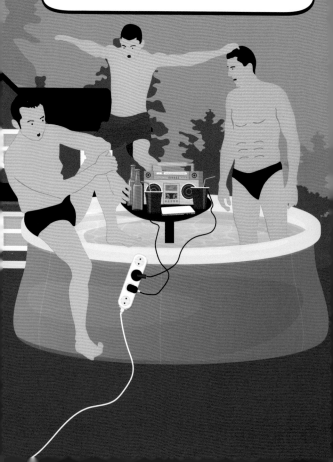

In South Africa, a rhino poacher found his extinction after he

TRESPASSED INTO A NATIONAL PARK.

With the intention of killing a rhino for it's horn, this cruel man was

TRAMPLED BY AN ELEPHANT, THEN DEVOURED BY A LION. 1-0 TO WILDLIFE!

MIXING WATER WITH ELECTRICITY MEANS ONE THING - DANGER!

Despite obvious warning signs, a 36 year old English man decided it would be a bright idea to plug his iPhone charger into an extention, and

USE HIS PHONE WHILE IN THE BATH!

Resting the charger on his chest, he received terrible burns, but not before succumbing to heart failure due to electrocution!

In Cambodia, three friends shared a drink and engaged in playful argument with one another. Finding a crazy solution to end the argument,

ONE OF THE MEN PLACED AN UNEXPLODED LANDMINE UNDER THE CAFÉ TABLE,

and the men took turns downing a drink and stomping on it. Everyone else left the cafe in horror, and needless to say,

THE MINE WENT KABOOM!

Women would just agree to disagree.

Dressed as Dracula, a college student wanted to make his outfit realistic by adding a real stake through the heart. With a thin wooden board under his shirt, he

HAMMERED A KNIFE INTO HIS CHEST,

and in shock, staggered to his friends for help. He'd overestimated the thickness of the board, and

SUCCUMBED TO A STAKE THROUGH THE HEART!

A 25 year old Canadian man was dared by his drunk friends to go down the 'in-house water slide'.

What they actually meant was to

SLIDE 12 STOREYS DOWN THE GARBAGE CHUTE!

He accepted the challenge, sliding fast down the chute. What he and his friends didn't expect was a

WORKING TRASH COMPACTOR AT THE BOTTOM...

HOW NOT TO TRANSPORT GOODS